This Magnetic Woman Journal

Belongs to the Beautiful:

_____

Date received:

_____

www.MagneticWomanCoaching.com

Magnetic Woman™
Copyright © 2020 Tabatha Pittman
All rights reserved. No part of this publication may be reproduced, distributed, or transmitted in any form or by a means, including photocopying, recording, or other electronic or mechanical methods, without the prior written permission of the publisher, except in the case of brief quotations embodied in critical reviews and certain other noncommercial uses permitted by copyright law. For permission requests, write to the publisher, addressed "Attention: Permissions Coordinator," at the email address below.
Email requests to info@TabathaPittman.com.
Ordering Information:
Quantity sales. Special discounts are available on quantity purchases by corporations, associations, and others. For details, contact the publisher at the email address above.
Published by Tabatha Pittman Coaching & Consulting LLC
Printed in USA
First Printing, 2020
ISBN:
ISBN-13:978-1-7356572-1-9

www.MagneticWomanCoaching.com

Prayers for My Family

DATE   **NAME**

Be Still and Know That I'm With You...
Psalm 46:10

www.MagneticWomanCoaching.com

Prayers for Myself

DATE	REFLECTIONS

Prayers For My Friends

DATE **NAMES**

For with God, nothing is impossible...

Prayers For my loves

DATE　　　　　　　　　　　　　**NAME**

My Prayer

www.MagneticWomanCoaching.com

DATE / /

Prayer JOURNAL

PERSONAL REFLECTIONS

Spiritual Inspiration

" I can do All **THINGS** through **CHRIST** WHO STRENGTHENS ME "

– PHILIPPIANS 4:13 –

www.MagneticWomanCoaching.com

DATE / /

Sermon JOURNAL

WHAT I LEARNED TODAY

Notes:

" The God of my ROCK in Him will I TRUST "

- 2 SAMUEL 22:3 -

www.MagneticWomanCoaching.com

DATE / /

Sermon JOURNAL

WHAT I LEARNED TODAY

Notes:

"*I will walk by* **FAITH** *even when I can't* **SEE**"

- 2 CORINTHIANS 5:7 -

www.MagneticWomanCoaching.com

DATE / /

Sermon JOURNAL

WHAT I LEARNED TODAY

Notes:

" *Be Still in the Presence of the* **LORD** *and wait patiently for him to act.* "
— PSALM 37:7 —

www.MagneticWomanCoaching.com

DATE / /

Sermon JOURNAL

WHAT I LEARNED TODAY

Notes:

"I Praise You
BECAUSE
I AM
fearfully and wonderfully
MADE"

— PSALM 139:14 —

www.MagneticWomanCoaching.com

DATE / /

Sermon JOURNAL

WHAT I LEARNED TODAY

Notes:

I AM GRATEFUL FOR

www.MagneticWomanCoaching.com

DATE / /

Sermon JOURNAL

WHAT I LEARNED TODAY

Notes:

" *By his wounds* we are **HEALED** "
- ISAIAH 53:5 -

I AM GRATEFUL FOR

www.MagneticWomanCoaching.com

Prayer Requests

DATE　　　　　　　　　　　　　　**NAMES**

Prayer Card　　　　　　　　　　　*Prayer Card*

www.MagneticWomanCoaching.com

Hymn Study

HYMN:

Favorite Verse

Lyrics of Faith

Sing to him, Sing praise to him, tell of all his wonderful acts.
Psalm 105:2

www.MagneticWomanCoaching.com

sermon NOTES

DATE / /   **TOPIC:**

SPEAKER: **PLACE OF WORSHIP:**

SCRIPTURE   **NOTES**

Key Points

www.MagneticWomanCoaching.com

sermon TRACKER

DATE

SCRIPTURE

NOTES

Reflections

www.MagneticWomanCoaching.com

DATE _____

Today's stand-out verse: *I am thankful for:*

Prayer Requests: *Inspirational Scripture:*

www.MagneticWomanCoaching.com

sermon NOTES

DATE / /   **TOPIC**

Scripture

Prayer & Praise

Personal Reflections

www.MagneticWomanCoaching.com

sermon NOTES

DATE

SERMON

Scripture

Notes

Be on your guard; stand firm in the faith; be courageous; be strong.
1 Corinthians 16:13

www.MagneticWomanCoaching.com

Sermon NOTES

DATE / /   **TOPIC:**

SPEAKER: **PLACE OF WORSHIP:**

Key Points

In **GOD** *we trust*

DATE:

This week I will focus on:

What I am most grateful for:

www.MagneticWomanCoaching.com

In GOD *we trust*

DATE:

This week I was most blessed by:

My calling in life is:

www.MagneticWomanCoaching.com

In GOD *we trust*

DATE:

My favorite passage of scripture is:

God is leading me to make the following changes:

www.MagneticWomanCoaching.com

In GOD *we trust*

DATE:

I feel God's presence most when:

What brings me the most joy is:

In GOD we trust

DATE:

My spiritual gifts are:

My enthusiasm for the gospel is increased when:

www.MagneticWomanCoaching.com

In **GOD** *we trust*

DATE:

One way I can apply the gospel to my life is:

An act of obedience God is prompting me to take is:

www.MagneticWomanCoaching.com

My time with the LORD

DATE:

Scripture that inspired me today:

Dear Lord:

www.MagneticWomanCoaching.com

www.MagneticWomanCoaching.com

www.MagneticWomanCoaching.com

Prayers for My Family

DATE   **NAME**

Be Still and Know That I'm With You...
Psalm 46:10

www.MagneticWomanCoaching.com

Prayers for Myself

DATE   **REFLECTIONS**

www.MagneticWomanCoaching.com

Prayers For My Friends

DATE **NAMES**

For with God, nothing is impossible...

www.MagneticWomanCoaching.com

Prayers For my loves

DATE   **NAME**

My Prayer

www.MagneticWomanCoaching.com

DATE / /

Prayer JOURNAL

PERSONAL REFLECTIONS

Spiritual Inspiration

" I can do All THINGS through CHRIST WHO STRENGTHENS ME "

- PHILIPPIANS 4:13 -

www.MagneticWomanCoaching.com

Sermon JOURNAL

DATE / /

WHAT I LEARNED TODAY

Notes:

"The GOD of my ROCK in Him will I TRUST"

- 2 SAMUEL 22:3 -

www.MagneticWomanCoaching.com

DATE / /

Sermon JOURNAL

WHAT I LEARNED TODAY

Notes:

> "I will walk by **FAITH** even when I can't **SEE**"
>
> — 2 CORINTHIANS 5:7 —

www.MagneticWomanCoaching.com

DATE / /

Sermon JOURNAL

WHAT I LEARNED TODAY

Notes:

> " *Be Still in the Presence of the* **LORD** *and wait patiently for him to act.* "
> — PSALM 37:7 —

www.MagneticWomanCoaching.com

Sermon Journal

DATE / /

WHAT I LEARNED TODAY

Notes:

"I Praise You BECAUSE I AM fearfully and wonderfully MADE"
- PSALM 139:14 -

www.MagneticWomanCoaching.com

Sermon JOURNAL

DATE / /

WHAT I LEARNED TODAY

Notes:

"Be Not Afraid, only BELIEVE"
— MARK 5:36 —

I AM GRATEFUL FOR

www.MagneticWomanCoaching.com

Sermon JOURNAL

DATE / /

WHAT I LEARNED TODAY

Notes:

"By his wounds we are HEALED"
- ISAIAH 53:5 -

I AM GRATEFUL FOR

www.MagneticWomanCoaching.com

Prayer Requests

DATE **NAMES**

Prayer Card *Prayer Card*

www.MagneticWomanCoaching.com

Hymn Study

HYMN:

Favorite Verse

Lyrics of Faith

Sing to him, Sing praise to him, tell of all his wonderful acts.
Psalm 105:2

www.MagneticWomanCoaching.com

sermon NOTES

DATE / /   **TOPIC:**

SPEAKER: **PLACE OF WORSHIP:**

SCRIPTURE   **NOTES**

Key Points

sermon TRACKER

DATE

SCRIPTURE

NOTES

Reflections

www.MagneticWomanCoaching.com

DATE

Today's stand-out verse: *I am thankful for:*

Prayer Requests: *Inspirational Scripture:*

www.MagneticWomanCoaching.com

sermon NOTES

DATE / /   **TOPIC**

Scripture

Prayer & Praise

Personal Reflections

www.MagneticWomanCoaching.com

sermon NOTES

DATE

SERMON

Scripture

Notes

Be on your guard; stand firm in the faith; be courageous; be strong.
1 Corinthians 16:13

www.MagneticWomanCoaching.com

Sermon NOTES

DATE / /   **TOPIC:**

SPEAKER: **PLACE OF WORSHIP:**

Key Points

In GOD we trust

DATE:

This week I will focus on:

What I am most grateful for:

www.MagneticWomanCoaching.com

In **GOD** *we trust*

DATE:

This week I was most blessed by:

My calling in life is:

www.MagneticWomanCoaching.com

In GOD *we trust*

DATE:

My favorite passage of scripture is:

God is leading me to make the following changes:

www.MagneticWomanCoaching.com

www.MagneticWomanCoaching.com

Prayers for My Family

DATE　　　　　　　　　　　**NAME**

Be Still and Know That I'm With You...
Psalm 46:10

www.MagneticWomanCoaching.com

Prayers for Myself

DATE **REFLECTIONS**

www.MagneticWomanCoaching.com

Prayers For My Friends

DATE **NAMES**

For with God, nothing is impossible...

www.MagneticWomanCoaching.com

Prayers For my loves

DATE **NAME**

My Prayer

www.MagneticWomanCoaching.com

DATE / /

Prayer JOURNAL

PERSONAL REFLECTIONS

Spiritual Inspiration

" I can do All THINGS through CHRIST WHO STRENGTHENS ME "

- PHILIPPIANS 4:13 -

www.MagneticWomanCoaching.com

DATE / /

Sermon JOURNAL

WHAT I LEARNED TODAY

Notes:

"The God of my ROCK in Him will I TRUST"

- 2 SAMUEL 22:3 -

www.MagneticWomanCoaching.com

Sermon JOURNAL

DATE / /

WHAT I LEARNED TODAY

Notes:

> "I will walk by **FAITH** even when I can't **SEE**"
>
> – 2 CORINTHIANS 5:7 –

www.MagneticWomanCoaching.com

DATE / /

Sermon JOURNAL

WHAT I LEARNED TODAY

Notes:

" *Be Still in the Presence of the* **LORD** *and wait patiently for him to act.* "

- PSALM 37:7 -

www.MagneticWomanCoaching.com

DATE / /

Sermon JOURNAL

WHAT I LEARNED TODAY

Notes:

"I Praise You BECAUSE I AM fearfully and wonderfully MADE"

- PSALM 134:14 -

www.MagneticWomanCoaching.com

Sermon JOURNAL

DATE / /

WHAT I LEARNED TODAY

Notes:

- MARK 5:36 -

I AM GRATEFUL FOR

www.MagneticWomanCoaching.com

Sermon JOURNAL

DATE / /

WHAT I LEARNED TODAY

Notes:

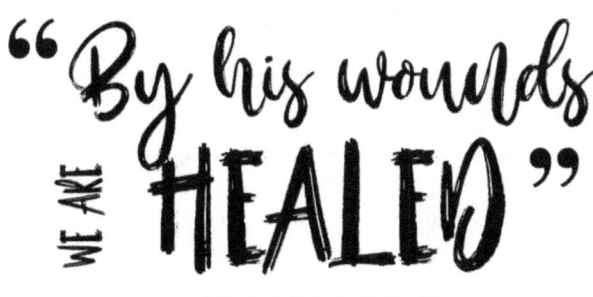
"By his wounds we are HEALED"
- ISAIAH 53:5 -

I AM GRATEFUL FOR

www.MagneticWomanCoaching.com

Prayer Requests

DATE   **NAMES**

Prayer Card   *Prayer Card*

www.MagneticWomanCoaching.com

Hymn Study

HYMN:

Favorite Verse

Lyrics of Faith

Sing to him, Sing praise to him, tell of all his wonderful acts.
Psalm 105:2

www.MagneticWomanCoaching.com

sermon NOTES

DATE / /   **TOPIC:**

SPEAKER: **PLACE OF WORSHIP:**

SCRIPTURE   **NOTES**

Key Points

www.MagneticWomanCoaching.com

sermon TRACKER

DATE

SCRIPTURE

NOTES

Reflections

www.MagneticWomanCoaching.com

DATE

Today's stand-out verse: I am thankful for:

Prayer Requests: Inspirational Scripture:

www.MagneticWomanCoaching.com

sermon NOTES

DATE / /   **TOPIC**

Scripture

Prayer & Praise

Personal Reflections

www.MagneticWomanCoaching.com

sermon NOTES

DATE

SERMON

Scripture

Notes

Be on your guard; stand firm in the faith; be courageous; be strong.
1 Corinthians 16:13

Sermon NOTES

DATE / /   TOPIC:

SPEAKER: PLACE OF WORSHIP:

Key Points

www.MagneticWomanCoaching.com

In GOD *we trust*

DATE:

This week I will focus on:

What I am most grateful for:

www.MagneticWomanCoaching.com

In GOD we trust

DATE:

This week I was most blessed by:

My calling in life is:

In GOD we trust

DATE:

My favorite passage of scripture is:

God is leading me to make the following changes:

www.MagneticWomanCoaching.com

www.MagneticWomanCoaching.com

Prayers for My Family

DATE **NAME**

Be Still and Know That I'm With You...
Psalm 46:10

www.MagneticWomanCoaching.com

Prayers for Myself

DATE	REFLECTIONS

www.MagneticWomanCoaching.com

Prayers For My Friends

DATE **NAMES**

For with God, nothing is impossible...

www.MagneticWomanCoaching.com

Prayers For my loves

DATE **NAME**

My Prayer

www.MagneticWomanCoaching.com

DATE / /

Prayer JOURNAL

PERSONAL REFLECTIONS

Spiritual Inspiration

" I can do All THINGS through CHRIST who STRENGTHENS ME "

- PHILIPPIANS 4:13 -

www.MagneticWomanCoaching.com

Sermon JOURNAL

DATE / /

WHAT I LEARNED TODAY

Notes:

> "The God of my Rock in Him will I Trust"
> – 2 SAMUEL 22:3 –

www.MagneticWomanCoaching.com

DATE / /

Sermon JOURNAL

WHAT I LEARNED TODAY

Notes:

" I will walk by **FAITH** even when I can't **SEE** "

- 2 CORINTHIANS 5:7 -

www.MagneticWomanCoaching.com

DATE / /

Sermon JOURNAL

WHAT I LEARNED TODAY

Notes:

" *Be Still in the Presence of the* **LORD** *and wait patiently for him to act.* "

— PSALM 37:7 —

www.MagneticWomanCoaching.com

DATE / /

Sermon JOURNAL

WHAT I LEARNED TODAY

Notes:

" I Praise You
BECAUSE
I AM
fearfully and wonderfully
MADE "

- PSALM 139:14 -

www.MagneticWomanCoaching.com

Sermon JOURNAL

DATE / /

WHAT I LEARNED TODAY

Notes:

"Be Not Afraid, only BELIEVE"
— MARK 5:36 —

I AM GRATEFUL FOR

www.MagneticWomanCoaching.com

Sermon JOURNAL

DATE / /

WHAT I LEARNED TODAY

Notes:

"By his wounds we are HEALED"
- ISAIAH 53:5 -

I AM GRATEFUL FOR

www.MagneticWomanCoaching.com

Prayer Requests

DATE **NAMES**

Prayer Card   *Prayer Card*

www.MagneticWomanCoaching.com

Hymn Study

HYMN:

Favorite Verse

Lyrics of Faith

Sing to him, Sing praise to him, tell of all his wonderful acts.
Psalm 105:2

www.MagneticWomanCoaching.com

sermon NOTES

DATE / / **TOPIC:**

SPEAKER: **PLACE OF WORSHIP:**

SCRIPTURE **NOTES**

Key Points

www.MagneticWomanCoaching.com

sermon TRACKER

DATE

SCRIPTURE

NOTES

Reflections

www.MagneticWomanCoaching.com

DATE

Today's stand-out verse:

I am thankful for:

Prayer Requests:

Inspirational Scripture:

www.MagneticWomanCoaching.com

sermon NOTES

DATE / /   **TOPIC**

Scripture

Prayer & Praise

Personal Reflections

www.MagneticWomanCoaching.com

sermon NOTES

DATE / /

SERMON

Scripture

Notes

Be on your guard; stand firm in the faith; be courageous; be strong.
1 Corinthians 16:13

www.MagneticWomanCoaching.com

Sermon NOTES

DATE / /   **TOPIC:**

SPEAKER: **PLACE OF WORSHIP:**

Key Points

In GOD we trust

DATE:

This week I will focus on:

What I am most grateful for:

www.MagneticWomanCoaching.com

In GOD *we trust*

DATE:

This week I was most blessed by:

My calling in life is:

www.MagneticWomanCoaching.com

In **GOD** *we trust*

DATE:

My favorite passage of scripture is:

God is leading me to make the following changes:

www.MagneticWomanCoaching.com

www.MagneticWomanCoaching.com

www.MagneticWomanCoaching.com

Prayers for My Family

DATE　　　　　　　　　　　　　　**NAME**

Be Still and Know That I'm With You...
Psalm 46:10

www.MagneticWomanCoaching.com

Prayers for Myself

DATE	REFLECTIONS

Prayers For My Friends

DATE **NAMES**

For with God, nothing is impossible...

www.MagneticWomanCoaching.com

Prayers For my loves

DATE **NAME**

My Prayer

DATE / /

Prayer JOURNAL

PERSONAL REFLECTIONS

Spiritual Inspiration

" I can do All THINGS through CHRIST who strengthens me "

- PHILIPPIANS 4:13 -

www.MagneticWomanCoaching.com

Sermon JOURNAL

DATE / /

WHAT I LEARNED TODAY

Notes:

> "The God of my ROCK in Him will I TRUST"
>
> - 2 SAMUEL 22:3 -

www.MagneticWomanCoaching.com

DATE / /

Sermon JOURNAL

WHAT I LEARNED TODAY

Notes:

" I will walk by **FAITH** even when I can't **SEE** "

— 2 CORINTHIANS 5:7 —

www.MagneticWomanCoaching.com

Sermon JOURNAL

DATE / /

WHAT I LEARNED TODAY

Notes:

> "Be Still in the Presence of the LORD and wait patiently for him to act."
> — PSALM 37:7 —

www.MagneticWomanCoaching.com

DATE / / # Sermon JOURNAL

WHAT I LEARNED TODAY

Notes:

" I Praise You
BECAUSE I AM
fearfully and wonderfully
MADE "
- PSALM 139:14 -

www.MagneticWomanCoaching.com

DATE / /

Sermon JOURNAL

WHAT I LEARNED TODAY

Notes:

I AM GRATEFUL FOR

www.MagneticWomanCoaching.com

Sermon JOURNAL

DATE / /

WHAT I LEARNED TODAY

Notes:

"By his wounds we are HEALED"
- ISAIAH 53:5 -

I AM GRATEFUL FOR

www.MagneticWomanCoaching.com

Prayer Requests

DATE **NAMES**

Prayer Card *Prayer Card*

www.MagneticWomanCoaching.com

Hymn Study

HYMN:

Favorite Verse

Lyrics of Faith

Sing to him, Sing praise to him, tell of all his wonderful acts.
Psalm 105:2

www.MagneticWomanCoaching.com

sermon NOTES

DATE / / **TOPIC:**

SPEAKER: **PLACE OF WORSHIP:**

SCRIPTURE **NOTES**

Key Points

www.MagneticWomanCoaching.com

sermon TRACKER

DATE

SCRIPTURE

NOTES

Reflections

www.MagneticWomanCoaching.com

DATE

Today's stand-out verse:

I am thankful for:

Prayer Requests:

Inspirational Scripture:

www.MagneticWomanCoaching.com

sermon NOTES

DATE / /   **TOPIC**

Scripture

Prayer & Praise

Personal Reflections

www.MagneticWomanCoaching.com

sermon NOTES

DATE

SERMON

Scripture

Notes

Be on your guard; stand firm in the faith; be courageous; be strong.
1 Corinthians 16:13

www.MagneticWomanCoaching.com

Sermon NOTES

DATE / /   **TOPIC:**

SPEAKER: **PLACE OF WORSHIP:**

Key Points

DATE / /   *Sermon* JOURNAL
___

WHAT I LEARNED TODAY

Notes:

> " I will walk by **FAITH** even when I can't **SEE** "
> — 2 CORINTHIANS 5:7 —

www.MagneticWomanCoaching.com

www.ingramcontent.com/pod-product-compliance
Lightning Source LLC
LaVergne TN
LVHW061333060426
835512LV00017B/2670